sport snaps
jeff gordon

chris Pronger

the captain

44

THIS SERIES OF BOOKS IS DEDICATED
TO BARCLAY PLAGER, THE TOUGHEST MAN
ANY OF US COULD EVER HOPE TO KNOW.

J.G.

PHOTO CREDITS:

Allsport
1 [T. Warshaw], 12 left [D. Pensinger],
32 bottom [B. Bahr].

BBS
Front Cover [J. McIsaac], 5 [J. Giamundo],
8 [S. Levy], 20 top [A. Foxall], 24 [J. Leary], 25 top
[B. Winkler], 25 bottom [B. Bennett], 27 [B. Bennett],
28 [J. McIsaac], 32 top [B. Bennett], 33 top and
bottom [B. Bennett], 37 middle [B. Bennett], 39 top
[B. Bennett], Inside Back Cover [J. McIsaac].

Mary Butkus
11 top and bottom, 12 bottom, 30, 31, 35,
36 bottom.

C. Melvin/RVP
10.

Detroit Free Press
34 bottom.

Mitchell Layton/RVP
38 top.

The Sporting News
Inside Front Cover, 6, 12 top, 13, 14, 22, 26 top
and bottom, 34 top, 37 top and bottom, 38 bottom,
39 bottom, 40.

Ron Vesely/RVP
36 top.

Photos courtesy of Chris Pronger: 3 top and
bottom, 4, 7, 16 top and bottom, 17, 18 top and
bottom, 19, 20 bottom, 21.

Jeff Gordon's photo courtesy of the
St. Louis Post-Dispatch.

© 1998 GHB Publishers, L.L.C.
All rights reserved.

Printed by Pinnacle Press, Inc.
in the United States of America.

Edited by Tami Lent.

Designed by Werremeyer Creative.

LIBRARY OF CONGRESS
CATALOG CARD NUMBER 98-88541

table of contents

the day

44

CHRIS PRONGER WILL NEVER FORGET

"It would probably be the NHL draft in 1993 (when Hartford selected him second overall, after Ottawa took Alexandre Daigle), because I had all my family and friends there. Just the fact that I had accomplished that part, and now I just had to get to the next level and get myself established. Growing up, only a few kids get that opportunity to get to that level and that happened for me. Now you move on to the next battle, to establish yourself in the NHL, to obviously improve and make the team.

"Certainly, I was the guy Hartford wanted to draft. San Jose had pretty much told me they weren't going to draft me at No. 2, or they would trade the pick. A few teams were trying to deal with San Jose to get me. There was a wide range of teams they were talking to, but in the end, it was Hartford."

CHRIS WITH HIS FATHER, JIM.

CHRIS PRONGER

profile

44

BORN:
OCT. 10, 1974,
DRYDEN, ONTARIO

FAMILY:
SINGLE

Favorite off-season diversions: "I pretty much just go out with my buddies fishing, golfing."

Getaway from hockey during the season: "I'm a big movie fan. I go home, watch a couple movies, chill out."

Movies you watch over and over again? "Sports movies like 'Slap Shot,' 'Major League,' 'Youngblood,' movies of that type. Suspense films, Mafia movies like 'Goodfellas.'"

Any TV addictions? "Other than I have it on all the time? I've got the dish, so I have East Coast and West Coast ABC, NBC, stuff like that. But there's nothing I HAVE to watch."

From the entertainment world, who makes you laugh? "I like Seinfeld, his humor. The Leslie Nielsen spoofs are pretty funny, too."

Are you a Net Boy? "A little bit. I'm trying to learn how to use the computer and do all that stuff."

Do you play the NHL '99 video game? "I try to stay away from the hockey games as much as possible. All my buddies play it back home. I play football and baseball on my Play Station."

What do you like most about St. Louis? "Probably the people. They are very friendly, easy to get along with. I think it's kind of a Midwest thing; the people are very open and cordial, even if they don't know you."

Any one book influence you? "I read books, but they are more biographies and business books. There hasn't been one book, like *Moby Dick*, to inspire me to do anything."

Any food you can't resist? "I guess I get cravings. I'll go two months without having a chocolate bar, then I'll be walking somewhere and it's, 'I've got to have six of those chocolate bars. Right now.'"

Keys to survival on the road: "It certainly helps to have a good roommate. I know in a lot of different sports, athletes tend to want their own room, but I think you go a little stir crazy in the room by yourself. You have to be out intermingling with the guys, having that camaraderie. It kills the monotony."

The music on your CD player? "Pretty much anything. I listen to country, rock, alternative. I'm not a big rap fan. Rap is pretty much the only music I won't listen to."

Back row: Sean, Chris, Jim and Eila Pronger.
Front row: Maternal grandparents Eric and Ann Nyholm.

Anybody you'd like to meet? "I don't think there is one person, in particular, I really want to meet. I'm sure there have been people through history I would have liked to have met."

" He's an excellent skater for a big guy.
He can handle the puck well. He can shoot the puck well.
He's got character, too.
He's got leadership ability. He's quiet, but he leads by example."

THEN-HARTFORD WHALERS GENERAL MANAGER BRIAN BURKE

CHRIS PRONGER WAS A SKINNY 16-YEAR-OLD THE FIRST TIME HARTFORD WHALERS SCOUT BRUCE HARALSON SAW HIM PLAY JUNIOR HOCKEY. WHAT IMPRESSED HARALSON WAS NOT PRONGER'S GREAT HEIGHT AND RANGE, BUT HIS DEMEANOR. "HE WAS SO COOL, SO AWARE OF WHAT HE WAS DOING ON THE ICE," HARALSON RECALLED A FEW YEARS LATER. "POISE."

second

NHL | second player selected in 1993 NHL Entry Draft

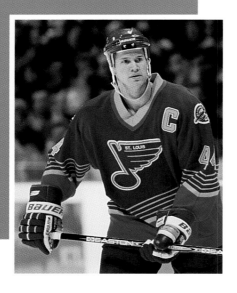

BUT WAS HE TOO COOL? Brian Burke was general manager of the Whalers when that team's hockey operation became smitten with Pronger before the 1993 draft. When Burke checked out Chris himself, he wondered if he was seeing grace under fire or nonchalance.

So it has always been for Chris Pronger. What hockey experts like most about him, his calmness amid crisis, has also invited skepticism. He didn't rush up and down the ice with the puck like a maniac. He didn't skate around crashing into anybody near the puck.

> "He has no idea how good he is. As good as he's played, he could be 10 times better. He could be a Norris Trophy winner in this league."
>
> DALLAS STARS WINGER BRETT HULL

Mostly, he played his position shift after shift, covered lots of ice and moved the puck out of danger. Other general managers and coaches made note of his growth more quickly than Blues fans or local media types picked up on it. His game consisted of little things, done well.

"Just because you're calm or whatever with the puck, just because you don't get rattled, that doesn't mean you don't care," Pronger says. "That was the biggest thing that ticked me off. People said, 'He doesn't care.' Well, sorry for being calm! I'm supposed to run around with my head cut off and get out of position?"

Chris Pronger's Tips for Young Players: DEVELOPING BETTER AGILITY AND SKATING ABILITY

"I THINK THE BIGGEST THING WHEN I FIRST STARTED WAS, I DIDN'T PLAY HOCKEY RIGHT AWAY. I TOOK SKATING LESSONS FOR A YEAR AND LEARNED HOW TO SKATE, LEARNED TO USE ALL MY EDGES. FROM THERE, I LEARNED THE GAME. I WAS ALWAYS SOMEWHAT COORDINATED. I NEVER WENT THROUGH A GEEKY STAGE WHERE I WAS FALLING ALL OVER THE PLACE. I WAS ALWAYS KIND OF BIG. I GOT USED TO BEING THAT SIZE. EVERY SUMMER BEFORE HOCKEY SEASON STARTED, MY BROTHER AND I WOULD GO TO A HOCKEY SCHOOL FOR ONE OR TWO WEEKS, DO THE SKATING, JUST TO GET USED TO PLAYING HOCKEY AGAIN."

+47

NHL | **1997-98 plus-minus leader (+47)**

When Pronger chose to stick with his friends and play high school hockey instead of midget hockey, some coaches questioned his commitment to the sport. He had no ambition to try major junior hockey, opting instead to play junior B hockey at Stratford. He hoped to play collegiate hockey like his older brother, Sean, who played at Bowling Green for four seasons before beginning his pro career.

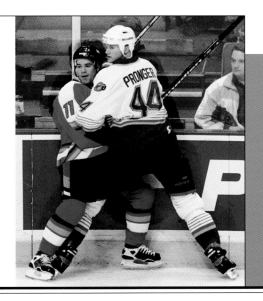

Was he indifferent? Hardly, as it turned out. He was stung by his rejection at a regional camp for the Canadian under-17 program, where his conditioning was questioned. He elevated his game, starring for Stratford before agreeing to join the Peterborough Petes, a major junior hockey powerhouse.

He would help lead the Petes to the Memorial Cup final. He would stand out in various national camps and international junior tournaments. He would help lead Canada to a gold medal in a world junior championship. He would earn all-star and top defenseman honors for both the OHL and the umbrella organization for major junior hockey in that country, the Canadian Hockey League. In his second season at Peterborough, he recorded an astonishing plus-minus rating of plus-92.

Burke's reservations quickly evaporated, and the Whalers took him second overall in the 1993 draft, behind flashy center Alexandre Daigle. Sure, Pronger was outwardly quiet. But Hartford saw real leadership potential. The intensity was there.

"We knew there would be some lag time. He's very intense.

You could see it in his demeanor as his confidence grew."

THEN-BLUES COACH MIKE KEENAN

Pronger starred as a first-year player, making the NHL's All-Rookie team, then suffered through a sophomore slump in the lockout-shortened 1994-95 season. Sensing Hartford's impatience (Burke was long gone, replaced by Jim Rutherford after an ownership change), St. Louis Blues general manager and coach Mike Keenan offered all-NHL left winger Brendan Shanahan for Pronger straight up in the summer of 1995.

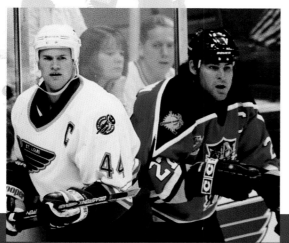

The deal was done and Pronger arrived in St. Louis amid catcalls, since Shanahan had been the franchise's most popular player. As gregarious and emotional as Shanahan was, Pronger seemed just that quiet and unaffected. His first season in St. Louis was a grim struggle, an ordeal that tested his resolve.

In time, though, he would assert himself and become a crowd-pleasing force. The transformation started in the 1996 playoffs, then continued through a summer of rigorous training and into the next season. He stood out in the 1997 playoff series with Detroit, then starred for Team Canada in the World Championships.

Blues coach Joel Quenneville showed the ultimate confidence in him the next fall, naming him captain of the team before his 23rd birthday. Just as Pronger rose to the top of major junior hockey, he proved he could rule the NHL on defense. "The way he has played the last couple of years," teammate Al MacInnis says, "his development has been second to none as far as young defensemen go."

Team Canada drafted him for the Winter Olympics in Nagano, Japan. He led the NHL in plus-minus at plus-47, was named a finalist for the Norris Trophy and was honored as the defenseman of the year by the *The Hockey News*.

"I had to adapt," Pronger says. "The physical part of the game has to be consistent and constant. I've been able to grasp that. Emotions run high out there, but you can't get too caught up in them. You can't lose your focus on your job out there. You can't let them get the best of you out there and let guys get you off your game. And when you have a chance to get a shot in, you've got to make it a good one."

Around the NHL, top coaches like Marc Crawford and Larry Robinson raved about his work. And, finally, the fans of St. Louis came around. The whipping boy became a hero. The stands started filling up with fans wearing No. 44 sweaters.

"It certainly stinks to be booed," Pronger says. "But it's certainly a nice feeling when the fans are behind you and they enjoy the way you play."

1993-94

NHL | **named to 1993-94 All-Rookie team**

BLUES FANS WOULD BE SURPRISED TO KNOW PRONGER WASN'T ALWAYS ONE COOL KID. GROWING UP IN DRYDEN, ONTARIO — A PULP AND PAPER TOWN OF ABOUT 7000, SITUATED 3 AND ONE-HALF HOURS NORTHWEST OF THUNDER BAY — JIM AND EILA'S YOUNGEST BOY WOULD GET A BIT, WELL, IMPATIENT WITH SOME OF HIS PLAYMATES.

captain

BLUES | named team captain on September 29, 1997

"MY NICKNAME BACK HOME WAS 'CHAOS,'" Pronger says. "I was a little bit of a hellion. I was a little crazy as a kid. I still am at times. I have to watch myself."

He and his older brother, Sean, who would also reach the NHL, weren't adverse to roughhousing. "Yeah, we killed each other a little bit," Chris says. "That was the saying back home: 'There go the Prong boys again.'"

The battles started in their basement on Saint Charles Street. A couch cushion was moved to create a goal. With hockey sticks and a plastic puck, the lads went to war. "Chris would always be on defense, and I'd always be on offense," Sean says. "We'd play one-on-one hockey down there for a long time. As we got older, it got more and more competitive. Pretty soon, we wouldn't play anymore because we were always fighting."

(Later, Eila and Jim got to see the boys face each other in the NHL. Mom wore a Mighty Ducks sweater, Dad wore a Blues sweater. "And I was hoping one wouldn't bump into the other and start something," Eila says.)

IN THE 1984-85 SEASON, CHRIS AND SEAN PLAYED ON THE SAME TEAM. SEAN WAS CAPTAIN; CHRIS IS IN THE FIRST ROW, SECOND TO THE LEFT.

You couldn't miss these boys around Dryden. Chris, who grew up to stand 6 feet 6 inches and weigh 220 pounds, said he was the tall kid for as long as he could remember. Sean, now 6 feet 2 inches and 205 pounds, was always one of the bigger kids, too.

"I THINK THE BIGGEST THING IS NOT REALLY PAYING A LOT OF ATTENTION TO THE PUCK. GUYS HOLD IT OUT THERE, THEN COME BACK HERE. YOU WANT TO TRY TO STAY IN POSITION AND LET THE OPPONENT MAKE HIS MOVE. THEN YOU GO PLAY HIM. BE PATIENT. A LOT OF TIMES, GUYS THINK, 'I'VE GOT TO HIT HIM!' YOU CAN GET OVERAGGRESSIVE AND MISS, AND THE GUY WILL BE GOING IN ON A BREAKAWAY. YOU'VE GOT TO BE PATIENT AND LET HIM MAKE HIS MOVE."

Predictably, sports were a large part of their life. Chris, who is two years younger than Sean, started skating at 4 and playing hockey at 5.

There were regular road hockey games outside their home. Up the street was an outdoor hockey rink that was most popular; the kids would start skating shortly after school, and the gang would organize games at night. Chris figures he learned his puckhandling skills during these pick-up games. "Once you get into team hockey, that's where you learn how to play the game, the team-oriented skills," he says. "Most guys who are gifted with the puck, they played a lot of street hockey, summer hockey, just fooling around."

But in league play, Chris didn't fool around. "I was really competitive as a kid. I used to get ticked off," he says. "Playing Atom hockey, kids obviously aren't going to be as good. These kids are 6, 7 years old. I'm out there screaming and hollering. Kids were scared of me, because I'd get so mad. You learn from stuff like that."

Like Sean, Chris started out as a big center who could score. He recalls putting away 130 goals one season. But during his first season of Atom hockey, his team only had two lines of forwards, three defensemen and a goaltender. So the next season, he switched to defense because he figured he'd seldom come out of games. He was right. He didn't.

That position switch would pay off handsomely down the road. The NHL covets big defensemen, especially if they have any agility at all. Pronger was never really awkward; his game developed smoothly as he grew. And as he matured, he started to outgrow some of his tantrums.

He started to realize how absurd he must look during games. "When I was in Grade 6, playing baseball, I'd be screaming at kids, 'What are you doing? Throw the ball! Come on!' I was so wound up," he says. "After that, you think, 'Was it really worth it, getting that upset?' You can't control anybody else but you. That's kind of the way I've adapted my thinking. This is where I got a little more laid back.

"Obviously, you'd get mad once in a while. I still yell, don't get me wrong."

Pronger was reluctant to venture onto hockey's fast track. He eschewed midget hockey to play with his buddies for two years of high school. Then he went off to play junior B hockey at Stratford, Ontario, just before his 16th birthday.

Playing in the rugged Western Hockey League didn't sound appealing, and he wasn't enamored with the Ontario Hockey League either. He told any scout who asked exactly how he felt. When Peterborough Petes coach Dick Todd called to inform him he'd been drafted in the sixth round of the OHL draft anyway, he was nonplussed.

"I said, 'Oh, yeah.' He's on the phone, waiting for me to say, 'Oh, thanks,' and I said, 'Oh, yeah.' I had no intention of going there," Pronger says. "Especially from up there in Dryden, you hear all the stereotypes, that it's "goon" hockey. You don't really see any of the hockey, you don't know anybody who has ever played there. You just hear the horror stories and the rumors of what the league is like. You don't know what to expect. That's one of the things Dick Todd was pushing, to just go down there and see how it was."

103

NHL | career assists: 103

"First and foremost, he's a defensive defenseman.

He's got a great stick, and he's really smart. He could play the whole game. I'm sure as he gets older, you'll see him playing 40 minutes a game like Ray Bourque in his prime."

PHILADELPHIA FLYERS COACH ROGER NEILSON

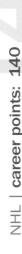

NHL | career points: 140

Todd had seen Pronger star at an under-18 international tournament in Japan. Before that, Pronger had held his own with Canada's other stars in under-17 competition. Todd kept after him. Why didn't he want to play major junior hockey?

Pronger finally relented. He ventured down to Peterborough and wasted no time becoming one of the top players in the league. "I was practicing every day, playing every day, just getting the ice time to improve and develop," Chris says. "The competition level is great. You have to keep going up the ladder, to keep improving. I always caught on quickly and kept going."

Burke figures Chris learned quite a bit from watching Sean go through the hockey paces. Burke was director of hockey operations for the Canucks when the club drafted Sean 51st overall in the 1991 draft.

Sean played junior hockey for Thunder Bay in the United States Hockey League, then played at Bowling Green for four seasons. He blossomed into a solid collegiate scorer, netting a total of 40 goals in his last two seasons, but the Canucks chose not to sign him.

CHRIS' BROTHER, SEAN.

So Sean had to battle his way into the NHL, starting in the East Coast Hockey League in 1994-95. The Mighty Ducks of Anaheim signed him as a free agent late that season – Anaheim general manager Jack Ferreira happened to see him play in Knoxville while in that city visiting family – and Sean reached the NHL the following season. He was traded to the Pittsburgh Penguins late in the 1997-98 season.

"It takes a number of years to learn to play defense in this game, and the hardest thing to do early in a career is to be consistent.

He very seldom
makes the wrong play.

He's smart because he makes the easy play, the right play.
If the winger's open, bang, he gives it to him.
For a defenseman, half the job is moving the puck out of his zone.
If the puck isn't in his zone, he's not going to get scored on."

BLUES DEFENSEMAN AL MACINNIS

Burke predicted Chris' path to the NHL might be smoother. "Generally speaking, the No. 2 brother in a hockey-playing family has a higher ratio of success than the No. 1," Burke said after drafting Chris for the Whalers.

Sean realizes Chris traveled a smoother path because of his talent. "I was his biggest fan growing up," he says. "I knew he was that much better than me. Even when we were younger, he was unbelievable."

three

NHL | career playoff goals: 3

Chris had been planning to follow Sean's lead to college, not necessarily to Bowling Green but to a program where he could continue developing his skills. Once he got to Peterborough, though, his career blasted off. Some scouts believe he would have gone in the top five of the 1992 draft, had he been old enough.

He got invited to Team Canada's camp for the world junior championships as a 17-year-old, allowing him to match up against stars like Eric Lindros. The next season he helped lead that squad to the gold medal in Sweden and led Peterborough to the Memorial Cup final.

A star was born. Todd would later say Pronger was the best player he ever coached, and he had superstars like Steve Yzerman and Larry Murphy. Whalers scout Leo Boivin, a Hall of Fame defenseman in his own right, called him the best defenseman to emerge from junior hockey since Denis Potvin.

"It's almost like a personal challenge when guys get in his kitchen a little bit."

BLUES WINGER KELLY CHASE

THE WHALERS WANTED PRONGER BADLY IN THE 1993 ENTRY DRAFT. WHEN HARTFORD SCOUTS WERE ASKED TO NAME THE TOP PROSPECT IN THE DRAFT POOL, THEY VOTED UNANIMOUSLY FOR PRONGER.

BURKE ENGINEERED A DEAL WITH THE SAN JOSE SHARKS (WHO COVETED BIG CENTER VIKTOR KOZLOV) TO TRADE UP FROM SIXTH IN THE FIRST ROUND TO SECOND. THERE WAS MUCH INTRIGUE LEADING UP TO THE PICK. "THE RANGERS WERE IN IT, QUEBEC WAS IN IT," BURKE SAID. "WHEN THE PRICE WAS GOING UP, I SAID TO THE SCOUTS, 'NO GUTS, NO GLORY. LET'S GO FOR IT.'"

eighteen

NHL | **career playoff points: 18**

COACH PAUL HOLMGREN COULD SCARCELY CONTAIN HIS EXCITEMENT when the deal got done. "I'm just lucky I'm wearing a dark suit," he quipped on draft day.

Pronger was a bit surprised to become a Whaler. Tampa Bay seemed better positioned to deal with San Jose, so he figured he'd be joining the Lightning. Hartford? He had no idea that team would climb up the draft ladder and get him.

Chris Pronger's
Tips for Young Players:
MOVING THE PUCK OUT
OF THE DEFENSIVE ZONE

"AGAIN, I THINK IT'S PATIENCE. LET THE PLAY DEVELOP. GUYS ARE GOING TO BE INTERMINGLING, AND HOLES ARE GOING TO BE OPENING UP. THERE IS ALWAYS AT LEAST ONE HOLE IN THE FORECHECK SOMEWHERE. YOU HAVE TO LET YOUR PLAYERS FIND THE HOLE AND MOVE IT TO THE HOLE. IF THEY DON'T, JUST SHOOT IT OUT OFF THE GLASS. IT'S SIMPLE. YOU HAVE TO BE PATIENT AND MAKE THE SIMPLE PLAY. YOU CAN'T LOOK FOR THE BREAKAWAY PASS ALL THE TIME. THE SIMPLE PASS IS EASIER."

#5

Other NHL personnel wizards congratulated the Whalers. Boston Bruins general manager Harry Sinden, not one to toss praise about casually, actually agreed that Pronger could be another Ray Bourque. "Of course, it's 15 years after the fact," Sinden said. "But he's got a real chance to be an all-star in this league."

Quebec Nordiques general manager Pierre Page compared the kid to legendary Montreal Canadiens defenseman Larry Robinson and tipped his cap to Burke. "All I know is, call me three years from now and you'll realize the impact of this trade," said Page, who reportedly offered San Jose an unsigned prospect named Peter Forsberg for a crack at Pronger. "You won't believe it. [The Sharks] just gave away Larry Robinson."

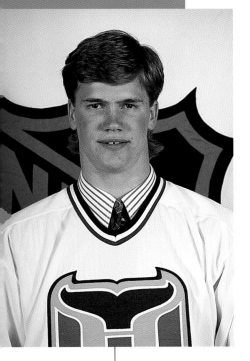

Burke tried to downplay all this "next Larry Robinson" stuff and keep the heat off Pronger. "The job of 'saving the franchise' is mine, not his," Burke said at the time. "There's no hype here. My timeline on Chris is 15 years, not 15 months."

Daigle was a marquee player, a speedy forward with great scoring potential. Pronger was a loping defender with merely fair offensive skills. Burke cautioned fans that Chris was not the sort of player who would bring folks out of their seats. He would not sell tickets all by himself, as spectacular scorers do.

Veteran defenseman Brad McCrimmon teamed with Pronger for two seasons in Hartford and quickly understood his real value. "A big reason for his development as a young player is his determination," McCrimmon says. "Chris has an interest in learning the game, and it showed when he broke in with Hartford. He asked questions and wanted to get better. He wanted to know why things happened and simply loved to learn."

That aspect of his personality was overlooked by fans and the media. "Certainly you come into the league with high expectations," Pronger says. "I think of myself as my own worst critic. I know when I've played a bad game. I know the things I really need to improve on. Just during the course of a game, I know the mistakes that I've made and I try to correct them."

But Pronger never got to be Hartford's cornerstone player. The lockout-shortened 1994-95 season was a fiasco for Pronger, the beginning of his end as a Whaler. He had stayed in Hartford for most of the summer, working out and preparing for training camp. He believed he was prepared for a big season . . . and then the lockout hit. Because he went back to Northwest Ontario and forgot about hockey in the months that followed, questions about his commitment to the game would arise again.

"I didn't do anything for three months but have a good time," he admits. "I came back in awful shape. I separated my shoulder in the first game, I think it was my second shift. I was out for two weeks and trying to get back in shape. I rushed myself back."

Chris Pronger's
Tips for Young Players:
GETTING YOUR SHOT
THROUGH THE DEFENSE
AND ON GOAL

#16

"THAT'S HUGE. IF YOU'VE GOT A FORWARD IN FRONT OF THE NET GETTING POUNDED ON, HE EXPECTS TO GET REWARDED A LITTLE BIT, AT LEAST GET A REBOUND. YOU'VE GOT TO USE HIM TO YOUR ADVANTAGE JUST BY WRISTING IT THROUGH. HE'S CREATING A SCREEN, OR TRAFFIC. A LOT OF TIMES THE GOALIE WILL BOBBLE IT. SOMETIMES THE PUCK WILL JUST BE LAYING THERE, AND THE GUY WHO WAS JUST GETTING BEAT ON GETS AN EMPTY NET GOAL. YOU'VE GOT TO JUST GET IT BY THE GUY COMING OUT ON YOU, WHETHER IT'S RIGHT BY HIS SHIN PAD OR BETWEEN HIS LEGS. IT'S SOMETHING THAT'S SOMETIMES OVER-LOOKED. GROWING UP, GUYS WANT TO TRY THE BIG AL MACINNIS SLAP SHOT."

> "He's turned into a great defenseman. He's had the potential for a long time and he's played for a long time, considering his age.
>
> # As he matures,
> ## he's going to get better and better.
>
> He has accepted the fact he's a leader, and he's fit that role well. He's got some meanness to him. A guy that big and having a little meanness – it's going to get him a little bit of respect around the league. That's going to make him more of a force."
>
> BLUES GOALTENDER GRANT FUHR

Whalers fans were not happy. They could sense their franchise was becoming a lame duck. Peter Karmanos, a Michigan-based computer mogul, had bought the club before the 1994-95 season and began questioning Hartford's viability as an NHL market. Pronger, who was supposed to be the symbol of a better future, became the target of "boo birds."

"Now I was really getting harassed in the city," he says. "I was supposed to be the savior."

Brendan Shanahan was a flashy performer capable of selling tickets and providing instant impact. Whalers general manager Jim Rutherford, who had replaced Burke with the ownership change, jumped at the chance to get him in exchange for Pronger. "I don't have the same disappointment in Pronger that maybe some of the fans and media do," Rutherford said at the time. "I think Chris is right on track, and maybe I'm one of his biggest supporters. I believe he is going to be a very, very good player."

Rutherford was correct. Shanahan would last a little more than a year in Hartford, and the Whalers would depart for North Carolina after two seasons. Pronger, meanwhile, would become a bulwark for the defensive-minded Blues. "With everything that happened over the course of my first few years," Pronger says, "I grew up pretty quickly and learned a lot on and off the ice."

But his education was just beginning.

1995

BLUES | acquired by trade from Hartford on July 27, 1995

" Look at how he got butchered when he got [to St. Louis].
To overcome all that pressure and all that negative response,
not because he's a bad guy, but because
how greatly loved Brendan Shanahan was . . .
it shows how mentally tough he is."

DETROIT RED WING POWER FORWARD DARREN McCARTY

PRONGER WAS COMPLETELY UNPREPARED FOR WHAT HE FACED IN
ST. LOUIS IN THE FALL OF 1995. HE KNEW SHANAHAN WAS POPULAR
IN TOWN, BUT HE DIDN'T REALIZE SHAN THE MAN WAS HOCKEY DEITY.
ALSO, HE HAD NO IDEA OF JUST HOW DEMANDING KEENAN WAS.

1998

NHL | **1998 Norris Trophy finalist**

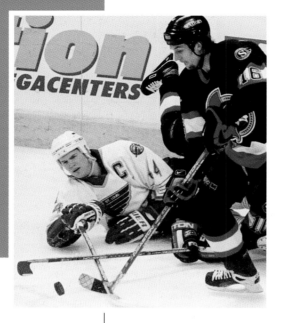

AFTER TOUTING PRONGER AS A FUTURE NORRIS TROPHY WINNER in the summer, Keenan ripped into him for showing up for camp in poor shape. Once again, Pronger seemed too easy going for his own good. His so-so performance in the wake of the big trade made him the object of much derision at Kiel Center.

"I'm bummed out about the previous year," Pronger says. "I'm getting booed. I go home, I don't do anything again. I barely work out again. I'm really in the dumps. I get traded to St. Louis, and now I'm getting booed again. Mentally, being booed constantly every time I got out there didn't help. I just kept getting buried deeper and deeper."

Pronger could have won some fans over by playing a more foolhardy, emotional game. A few monstrous hits, a few tooth-and-nail fights and Blues fans might have started to warm up to him. St. Louis adores fierce warriors.

But Chris refused to yield to public opinion and play somebody else's game. He was willing to hit, but he had no intention of bolting out of position to rock somebody. He wanted to play winning hockey, and he figured sooner or later the victories would win fans over. With him struggling and the team struggling, he was wondering if he'd EVER see the sun come up in St. Louis.

362

NHL | career games played: 362

> "He really struggled his first year [here in St. Louis]. I think he persevered through the tough times, and now **he's really shining out there. Every game he's been awesome for us.**"

Chris Pronger's Tips for Young Players:
PROVIDING LEADERSHIP FOR YOUR TEAM

"ANYTIME YOU HAVE A SUCCESSFUL TEAM, IT'S BECAUSE PLAYERS ARE LOOKING OUT FOR ONE ANOTHER, MAKING SURE EVERYBODY IS UPBEAT AND READY TO PLAY. LOOK AT DETROIT LAST YEAR. THEY RALLIED AROUND VLADIMIR KONSTANTINOV AFTER HE WAS INJURED [IN A CAR ACCIDENT]. THEY REALLY PULLED TOGETHER AND HAD A SUCCESSFUL YEAR. IT'S SOMETHING THE GREAT TEAMS HAVE. THEY HAVE EVERYBODY STRIVING IN THAT ONE DIRECTION AND EVERYBODY CARING. IT'S A TEAM SPORT, GETTING EVERYBODY ON THE SAME PAGE, WORKING TOWARD THE SAME GOAL."

Pronger admits he lapsed into some self-destructive tendencies, problems that could have proven ruinous had he not snapped out of his funk. "For like the first four months, when I was getting booed, I was thinking, 'When is this going to end?'" he says. "Mike was driving me down, I've got people booing me, and now I'm driving myself down."

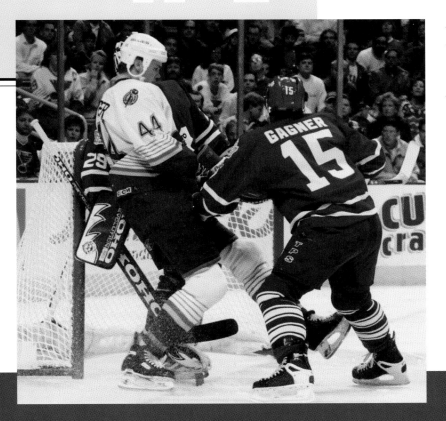

Some relief came in the form of Wayne Gretzky, whose arrival in the middle of the 1995-96 season turned the struggling Blues into a Stanley Cup contender. Pronger also did some soul-searching. "By March, I finally thought, 'To heck with everything. Just play,'" he says. "Don't worry about anything, just play."

The Gretzky-led Blues came inches from reaching the final four of the playoffs. Pronger was solid in the postseason, and the booing stopped. Finally, he could return home with his head up, feeling good about where his career was headed.

The 1996-97 season saw Pronger become one of the NHL's most underrated defensemen. He played solidly all season, peaking with an outstanding playoff. He earned a big workload, which, in turn, helped him regain some of the consistency he showed as a Whalers rookie. There was no time for his mind to wander. He would come off the ice, get a squirt of water, catch his breath and get back out there. Staying focused was much easier.

After the Blues bowed out of the playoffs in 1997, Pronger continued his progress by starring for Team Canada in the World Championships. He suffered a shoulder injury, which became a blessing when he hit the weight room to rehabilitate it. Calgary strength coach Charlie Polyquin put him and Sean through some rigorous paces. His body fat was a sportswriter-like 19 and one-half percent when he started working out in earnest, and it got down into single digits for training camp.

twenty-nine

NHL | career playoff games played: 29

A strong training camp gave him momentum into the season, when Pronger emerged as an elite NHL player. He became a monstrous presence on the blue line, helping drive the Blues to a fourth overall finish and a playoff victory over the Los Angeles Kings.

"Certainly things have kind of changed from the beginning of my career until now," Pronger says. "It takes time to mature and grow up and figure out where you want to be in the league. Do you want to be an average player? An elite player? An all-star? I had to get my head screwed on right and figure out what I wanted to do, that I didn't want to be average. As the years go by, you want to take a bigger role on the team."

A real highlight of his breakout season was his stint in the Olympics at Nagano, where he got to rub elbows with the greats of the game as a member of Team Canada. He saw the top players, how they carried themselves on and off the ice, how serious they were about hockey, how they wouldn't give an inch. Just by hanging around these guys, he learned plenty about leadership.

On the ice, Pronger made rival coaches drool with his ability to cover the defensive zone, turn back offensive rushes and move the puck back up the ice and out of danger. "Late in the game," Quenneville says, "he keeps the puck ahead of everyone. His anticipation is excellent for a young kid."

Increasingly, forecheckers found that going after Pronger was a waste of time. They come in to pressure him, and the puck passes them on the way up the ice. "Chris has a great first pass," Brad McCrimmon says. "As a result, he gets the puck moving right away, and the other team spends a lot less time in the St. Louis end of the ice."

Blues fans realized how much Pronger meant to them when he went down in the second-round playoff series against Detroit. A harmless looking shot caught him in the chest, disrupting his heartbeat. He collapsed to the ice at Joe Louis Arena and lay prone as doctors struggled to find a pulse. Jim and Eila Pronger raced down to ice level to be with him. Within a minute, his heart rate was back to normal – but he was hauled off to the hospital for precautionary tests.

MAY 10, 1998: CHRIS COLLAPSES AFTER BEING STRUCK BY THE PUCK.

> "Pronger is one of the top defensemen in the National Hockey League. He's here, playing with some of the best talent in the world in the Olympics, **and you can see he belongs with them.** And the thing about Chris is, as good as he is now, **he's only going to get better and better."**

FORMER COLORADO AVALANCHE AND
CANADIAN OLYMPIC HOCKEY COACH MARC CRAWFORD

"It's like I had a little nap, that's all," Pronger says. "It's not like I saw a light at the end of the tunnel or anything like that. There was no blinding light, no angels coming to take me home."

The tests underscored that he was fine, but the scare prompted an emotional response from Blues fans when he returned to action at Kiel Center in the next game. The roar told him that the city was finally prepared to embrace him.

"Every player wants to be recognized, to be a go-to guy that others are depending on," he says. "Certainly, those second and third years of my career, those were tough years. If you can get through stuff like that, I think it makes you a better person, a better player. Anytime I can get over struggles like that, to be able to turn it around and start playing the way I think I can play, keep striving to be the best, it's something I can be proud of."

1998

ANY PLAYERS YOU'D PAY TO WATCH PLAY?

"With Anaheim, Teemu Selanne and Paul Kariya together. When they are playing, that building should always be full. They are exciting to watch. So are Jaromir Jagr and Peter Forsberg. The combination they have there in Colorado with Joe Sakic, that's certainly something I'd want to watch. Wayne Gretzky still, obviously."

WHICH TEAMMATE HAVE YOU RESPECTED THE MOST?

"I think the guys who sit out for a prolonged period of time. Like last year, a Chris McAlpine sitting out 17 straight games at the start of the year and still being ready to come out and play that 18th game when he gets the call. When you have to sit out, that stinks. For them to stay upbeat, positive, be ready to come to the rink to play, that's tough."

WHICH OPPONENT HAVE YOU RESPECTED THE MOST?

"Certainly the Detroit rivalry. The battles we've had with Steve Yzerman, Sergei Fedorov – you could pretty much go up and down their whole lineup. Probably Peter Forsberg of Colorado. That's someone you get pumped up for. We kind of came into the league at the same time. Same with Paul Kariya. That's a kind of a rivalry that keeps going."

IS THERE ONE GUY YOU LEAST LIKE TO HAVE BEARING DOWN ON YOU?

"A guy who dumps the puck in my corner and I have to go get it . . . like Eric Lindros. There are times you HAVE to get the puck. If you bail out, he might score. You HAVE to get it out. If he's coming in and there's nobody holding him up, and you've got to get the puck out, you're probably going to be picking yourself off the ice."

IF YOU COULD BE COMMISSIONER FOR A DAY, WHAT CHANGES IN THE NHL GAME WOULD YOU MAKE?

"I think the biggest thing is to enforce the rules we have. If the officials call something, guys will stop doing it. I don't care if there are 40 penalties in that first game. Call it, the guys will stop doing it, and the game will start getting a flow. There will be more puck movement. It'll open up the game because guys won't be hooking and holding. Just enforce the rules the way they're supposed to be enforced."

WAS THERE ONE PERSON WHO MOST INFLUENCED YOUR CAREER?

"Probably my coach in junior hockey, Dick Todd. He worked hard to get me to go there. I wasn't really going to play major junior hockey. At that point, I was planning on going the scholarship route. He got me down there, showed me the lay of the land, the family I'd be staying with. He took me under his wing and really worked with me. The tradition of the Peterborough Petes is really something. There have been a lot of good hockey people go through there, like Bob Gainey, Steve Yzerman, guys like that."

Coach Joel Quenneville named Chris Pronger captain of the St. Louis Blues before the 1997-98 season, signifying the beginning of a new era. The franchise was building a new team and Pronger would be the cornerstone. Quenneville talks about the strengths Pronger brings to his team's defensive corps:

Skating in one-on-one against Chris is not a really easy assignment for a puck rusher.

"If Chris has good positioning on a guy one-on-one, the guy is not going to try to beat him, because of his long reach. You know you're going to have a pretty good chance of getting the puck poked away from you. Usually, players try to move to another lane or move the puck. One-on-one he's solid, with his reach and his size. It's tough to get around him. You have to have a hole and you've got to have high speed if you're thinking of entering his area."

Other big defensemen have trouble with their agility, with turning and skating backward, but Chris seems to cover the ice pretty easily.

"He moves well. Usually the big guys like that are clumsy. Actually, he skates solidly. He turns well, he pivots well. With that reach, he enables that turn to be wider. He covers a ton of space. He's agile for a big guy and when he's going, he's going pretty quickly."

He seems to have found a balance between keeping an edge to his game – letting people know he's back there – and being penalty prone.

"I think there's a fine line between knowing that you have to get some respect, and, at the same time, knowing you can't take undisciplined penalties. The opposition is going to be trying to get Chris off the ice, trying to annoy him – especially if they know he can be frustrated. I think he adapted last year, although there is still a process where his emotions have to be contained. He has to know when the right time is. There's been improvement in that area, but it's something you always have to guard against. At the same time, that uncertainty he can create in the other guys' minds [with physical play] is helpful."

He has become a steady presence on the ice.

"I think the ultimate test for a defenseman is consistency, and Chris has that. He's got a good head for the game, and for a young guy, that's amazing. His thought process and his anticipation are his greatest strengths."

He is pretty calm with the puck, a quality that comes with experience.

"He really is. When Chris has the puck, he's as good a passer as there is in the game. He can make that stick-to-stick, hard flat pass. He moves it well, and he sees the ice well. He sees all the options. His offensive numbers aren't huge, but at the same time, he knows he has to play defense first, then get involved in the attack. If we sent him more, his numbers would be higher."

His offensive asset is a good, low, hard, heavy shot.

"Chris has a good slap shot, but he has a really good wrist shot. His wrist shot gets through a lot, and it has a little bit of pace on it. To me, that's as good as a hard slap shot. A slapper, unless you've got a shot like Al MacInnis, seldom goes in the net, seldom beats a goaltender one-on-one. The wrist shot can be tipped, deflected, or there can be a rebound. To me, that's a dangerous shot. Denis Potvin lived off of that shot."

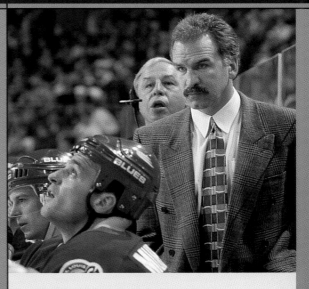

JOEL QUENNEVILLE SPENT 13 SEASONS IN THE NATIONAL HOCKEY LEAGUE, FLOURISHING AS A STAY-AT-HOME DEFENSEMAN FOR TORONTO, COLORADO, NEW JERSEY, HARTFORD AND WASHINGTON. IN 1991, QUENNEVILLE STARTED HIS SECOND CAREER BY BECOMING A PLAYER/ASSISTANT COACH FOR THE ST. JOHN'S MAPLE LEAFS IN THE AMERICAN HOCKEY LEAGUE.

QUENNEVILLE GRADUATED TO BECOME HEAD COACH OF THE AHL'S SPRINGFIELD INDIANS IN 1993-94. FROM THERE, HE JOINED THE QUEBEC NORDIQUES AS AN ASSISTANT COACH UNDER HEAD COACH MARC CRAWFORD. THE FRANCHISE MOVED TO DENVER FOR THE 1995-96 SEASON AS THE COLORADO AVALANCHE, AND QUENNEVILLE HELPED LEAD THE TEAM TO THE 1996 STANLEY CUP. ON JAN. 6, 1997, QUENNEVILLE LEFT COLORADO TO BECOME HEAD COACH OF THE BLUES. IN 1997-98, HE DIRECTED THE BLUES TO A SURPRISING 45-29-8 MARK — TYING THE TEAM FOR FOURTH OVERALL IN THE NHL STANDINGS.

QUENNEVILLE WAS BORN ON SEPT. 15, 1958, IN WINDSOR, ONT. HE AND HIS WIFE, ELIZABETH, HAVE THREE CHILDREN, DYLAN, LILY AND ANNA.

GAME-DAY routine

When the Blues play at home, here is what Chris Pronger's day will look like:

9 a.m. Ready or not, it's time to wake up, grab a little something to eat and head down to Kiel Center for the traditional game-day skate.

10 a.m. If Chris is feeling energetic that day, he'll do some preliminary work on his sticks for that night's game. If he is still dragging, he'll put off that task until he arrives at Kiel later in the day for the game. "It depends on how tired I am," he says. "If I get there early enough, I'll get my sticks made, but I won't have them taped or anything."

10:30 a.m. The Blues zip through a quick workout designed to keep them from getting stale on the day of the game. Since Pronger logs big minutes in the game, there is no reason to stay out and do extra skating. The players can also begin their mental preparations for the game by grabbing a printed breakdown of that night's opponent prepared by the team's video coordinator.

11:30 a.m. It's off to lunch, where Pronger has a similar meal on every game day. He's not one to eat a mid-day steak, chicken or slab of pork ribs. "I usually eat around noon," he says. "I have pasta, a couple bottles of water, usually some fruit. Always it's pasta."

12:30 p.m. Pronger, the movie buff, will dig into his video library, fish out one of his favorites and relax. Before long, his eyes will get heavy, he'll start to feel drowsy . . .

2 p.m. Nap time! Pronger always sleeps on the day of a game. "I try to get a little bit of sleep to calm myself down," he says. "I usually get an hour and a half."

3:30 p.m. It's time to wake up, pull himself together and head back to the Kiel Center to get ready for the game.

4:30 p.m. This is a good time to complete his stick preparation, if they aren't ready to go. "I tape up my sticks, curve them, do all that stuff," he says. "With the [soft] ice these days, I usually don't sharpen my skates that much. If there are some bad nicks, I'll get them done. But I don't really like my skates that sharp."

5:15 p.m. The Blues often hold special team meetings. As a key penalty killer and a point man on the power play, Pronger will always sit in on these strategy sessions.

5:30 p.m. The Blues coaching staff go over their scouting report for that night's opponent and briefly discuss the game plan for that night.

5:45 p.m. "After our meeting, I'll go stretch," Pronger says. "I'll kind of hang out in the back, watching TV, then I'll stretch at 6 p.m. and get dressed."

6:10 p.m. Unlike some of the more superstitious Blues, he has no detailed routine for getting dressed. "When I feel like getting dressed, I get dressed," he says. "I don't put equipment on any particular way. Sometimes I'll put on the right pads, then the right skates first. Other times I'm not paying attention, and I'll just throw it all on."

Also, Pronger doesn't have a specific routine for getting psyched up or more focused. "I don't sit there and veg out," he says. "I just go with the flow." Teammates like it when Chris is a little grouchy; this generally means he'll be on top of his game.

6:20 p.m. The Blues take the ice for a 20-minute warm-up. Some players like to linger at the end of warm-ups and do some solitary rituals with the puck; Pronger usually heads back to the dressing rooms with the pack.

7:05 p.m. Game time.

10 p.m. After the game, the players cool down their muscles by riding stationary bikes. Then they take medical treatments, park in the whirlpool, shower and then meet the press in their dressing area. The players head out in small groups to eat and relax.